Basic Lessons of Ministries

Published by Mesoamerica Region Discipleship Ministries

Translated into English from Spanish by: Monte Cyr

www.mesoamericaregion.org/en/discipleship-resources

ISBN: 978-1-63580-016-6

Printed in the United States

Table of Contents

Guide for the Discipler 2

Introduction to the Ministries of
the Local Church 6

Worship Ministries 10

Nazarene Compassionate Ministries 14

Communication Ministries 18

Personal Discipleship Ministry 22

Evangelism Ministries 26

Youth Evangelism Ministries 30

Youth Ministries (NYI) 34

Sunday School and Discipleship Ministries (SDMI).. 38

Nazarene Missions International (NMI) 42

Global Mission 46

Pastoral Ministries 50

Work and Witness 54

Certificate of completion 58

Guide for the
Discipler

Congratulations for having led your Christian brother or sister this far through the discipleship process, and now you're preparing to accompany him or her through the Basic Lessons of Ministries!

During the past months, you have been able to establish a close relationship of friendship with your disciple, helping to build a strong foundation for a new life in Christ. You have also probably grown much as well, and the process of discipleship continues. Now you will have the joy of helping your brother or sister discover the ministry or ministries in which they can be involved in their local church.

According to the scriptures, especially in the New Testament, God calls every one of his disciples to a ministry. In the church, Christ through his Holy Spirit, distributes a diversity of spiritual abilities known as Spiritual Gifts, to use in the service or ministry to others. These gifts are to be used by each Christian in the congregation to build up the church and extend the gospel to all who do not know Christ.

"There are different kinds of service, but the same Lord."
I Corinthians 12:5

"Tell Archippus: 'See to it that you complete the work you have received in the Lord.'"
Colossians 4:17

To facilitate the process of helping the new brother or sister know about the specific ministries in their local church, first look at each lesson to know them in general. Then you should share with him or her an introduction to the 12 lessons that give a general look at the following ministries:

- Worship
- Compassion (NCM)
- Communications
- Personal Discipleship
- Evangelism
- Youth Evangelism
- Nazarene Youth International (NYI)
- Sunday School and Discipleship Ministries International (SDMI)
- Nazarene Missions International (NMI)
- Global Mission (GMMAR)
- Pastoral Ministries
- Work and Witness (W&W)

You can take a lesson as an example and show the five sections of each one, oriented to his or her local church, explaining the following:

1. **What is this Ministry ...?** This is a concise statement that describes what the specific ministry of that lesson consists of.

2. **Using a Bible, answer the following questions:** The biblical basis of the ministry set forth in the lesson, which allows you to search the Bible and fill in the blanks as in the lessons of basic discipleship.

3. **What is the purpose of this ministry in my local church?** This indicates the reason this ministry exists in the local church. It is what the specific ministry seeks to bring to the total ministry of the church.

4. **How can this ministry benefit me in the development of my Christian life?** It shows how the fulfillment of this ministry will contribute to the growth and maturity of the faithful disciple of Jesus.

5. **Could I do this ministry?** This last section presents two important practical tools. First, it gives insights on how the ministry of the

lesson could be carried out if it is not yet being done in the local church. Second, it offers a questionnaire to see if the disciple could be trained or inclined toward the ministry presented in the lesson.

The lessons finish with a list of materials that you can use to qualify for this ministry. These additional resources will help you guide the new disciple to better know and develop the ministry indicated.

Suggested Methodology:

First, give the disciple the lesson: *Introduction to the Ministries in the Local Church* to complete.

Then you will need to help the disciple choose which ministry or ministry he or she feels inclined to. Usually, at the beginning people will choose based on their personal preference. Over time - and with the guidance of the Spirit - they will try different ministries, receive comments from other brothers and sisters and leaders, and this will help them discover their ministry. These lessons are meant to start this process. Feel free to share your perspectives on the possible ministries you envision that this brother or sister might do, since you have gotten to know him or her. However, remember that your opinions are not the final word. It is the Holy Spirit who confirms the ministry to which we are called.

If the disciple already knows which ministry or ministries they are most inclined toward, you can begin with those lessons. Since each lesson is a general and brief introduction, you could devote more than one session to understand well the ministry studied. For example, if you were doing the lesson on Nazarene Compassionate Ministries (NCM), in the first session you could guide them through the first three topics: What is NCM? Biblical basis and the purpose of NCM in the local church.

In a second session you could conclude with the last two topics: How can this ministry benefit you in your Christian life?

And how can NCM be developed in the local church? You can also review the ministry's questionnaire and look at possible additional materials.

If the disciple does not know what their ministry or ministries might be, you can guide them through all the lessons to discover their ministry. In any case, it would be good to study all the ministry lessons to get a general understanding of the possible ministries in which they can get involved.

It is advisable that during the course of the lessons, you invite the local ministry director for the ministry you are studying - if the ministry is active in the local church. This leader could share how he or she began in this ministry, their passion for this ministry, the blessings they have received and how this ministry has contributed to others. In addition, they should always be in conversation with the pastor so that he or she can guide them in any ministry from their own experience of Christian service.

You have embarked on a beautiful adventure of faith together with your new brother or sister in Christ. We encourage you to be consistent and allow God to use it powerfully. Ask the Lord to give you grace and wisdom to influence the life of your new sister or brother and so that you both can grow in your experience, knowledge and commitment to Christ and His church. Remember that you must aim for this disciple to become a trainer for other disciples.

Be a faithful and committed disciple and discipler of Jesus! It is our task for life!

— Discipleship Ministries, Mesoamerica Region Church of the Nazarene

discipleship@mesoamericaregion.org

Introduction
to the ministries of the
Local Church

This lesson...

- Will help you use Jesus' ministry as a model for ministry.
- Will show you that there is a diversity of ministries within the church.
- Will help you relate the ministry of the pastor in the local church to the ministries of the other brothers and sisters.
- Will motivate you to accept the call of being involved in one or more ministries of the church.

To memorize

"What, after all, is Apollos? And what is Paul? Only servants, through whom you came to believe—as the Lord has assigned to each his task. I planted the seed, Apollos watered it, but God has been making it grow. So neither the one who plants nor the one who waters is anything, but only God, who makes things grow. (I Corinthians 3:5-7).

Ministry in the local church

The word "ministry" literally means "service," but is a service by someone —a servant— who is a slave of others as Jesus was to all mankind. In the New Testament, the images of a rower or helper for someone superior are used referring to "servant."

I. The example for ministry in the church is Jesus.

Jesus' ministry was complete, and he touched all types of needs of humanity.

Let's look at what Luke 4:18-21 says about how Jesus saw his ministry.

The Spirit of the Lord is on_____, because he has _____ me to bring good news to the _____; he has sent me to proclaim _____ for the _____; recovery of _____ for the blind, and to set the _____ free; to proclaim the year of the Lord's _____.

a. What was the reaction of those who heard these words, according to Luke 4:22-29? _____
   _____
   _____
   _____

b. In Mark 10:45, what style did Jesus use in his ministry? _____
   _____
   _____

c. What important decision did Jesus make for his ministry, after praying, in Luke 6:12-16? _____
   _____
   _____

d. As he came to the end of his earthly ministry, what was the lesson that Jesus wanted to impress on the minds of his disciples in order that they might continue his ministry in the world, according to Luke 22:24-27 and John 13:4-5, 12-17?
   Luke 22:24-27: _____
   _____
   _____
   _____

   John 13:4-5, 12-17: _____
   _____
   _____

2. The diversity of Ministries in the Church

According to Acts 6:2-6, who were designated by the apostles to serve by waiting on the tables? _____

_____

_____

This passage is known as the official beginning of leadership in the church by laymen (people who weren't clergy). They did ministry alongside the apostles and were sent by them. So from very early in the life of the church, there were various ministries.

In I Corinthians 12:4-6, Paul used three categories to clarify to the Corinthians about the work of the Holy Spirit in the church:

Different kinds of g __ __ __ __ but the same Spirit.

Different kinds of s __ __ __ __ __ __ but the same Lord.

Different kinds of w __ __ __ __ __ __ but ... the same God.

Gifts are spiritual abilities that the Holy Spirit gives to each follower of Jesus, as He wants (I Corinthians 12:11), for the building up of the church (I Corinthians 14:12) in the fulfillment of His mission. "Working" refers to the results of the ministry of the church.

There are many passages in the New Testament that show the involvement of brothers and sisters, who weren't apostles, involved in the leadership of ministries. You can find examples in I Corinthians 16:15, Colossians 4:17, 2 Timothy 4:11.

3. Pastoral Ministry

Within the diversity of the ministries of the church, we have pastoral ministry. Some of the members of the church are gifted and called to be pastors of local congregations.

What would be the principle function of the pastor according to Ephesians 4:11-13? _____

_____

_____

In the original written language, in verse 11 the words "pastor and "teacher" go together to say Pastor-Teacher, giving the understanding that one of the principle functions of the pastor is to teach others so they can lead and participate in ministries in the church.

In 2 Timothy 4:5, what counsel related to ministry does Paul give to the young Pastor Timothy?_____

_____
_____
_____

What does Paul, who was a pastor among his other ministries, say in Acts 20:24 and 1 Timoteo 1:12 about his ministry?_____

_____
_____
_____
_____

Conclusion

The church as the body has been entrusted with the privilege of ministering to everyone, motivated by the love of Christ. Through the ministry of the pastor and the brothers and sisters, the local church is built and developed to reach out to many new disciples who still do not know Him. Thus, the true disciples of Jesus contribute their gifts and ministries to the total ministry of their local church. In this way, they continue growing and impacting others, locally and around the world, in order to "make disciples of all nations."

For this reason, we invite you to an adventure of participating in of or more ministries in the local church. As we have seen, that is the purpose of God for the life of his followers. God through his Holy Spirit wants to use you powerfully to serve others through the church. Accept the challenge and joy of allowing your life to make a difference in the lives of many others. As a faithful disciple of the Master, consecrate your life to serve others, together with your other brothers and sisters, in the name of Christ!

Worship
Ministries

I. What is Worship Ministries?

Worship Ministries is a ministry in the local church that guides us in the praise and worship that we give to God each time we gather as a congregation.

2. Using the Bible, answer the following questions:

a. According to John 4:23-24, How should true worshipers worship the Father? _____
_____
_____

b. What was the reaction of the people of Israel in 2 Chronicles 7:3 when they saw the fire of heaven and the glory of the Lord after Solomon's prayer to dedicate the temple? _____
_____
_____

c. What must be our rationale for worship, according to Romans 12:1? _____
_____
_____

d. What fruit should be produced in us who are filled by God's Holy Spirit, according to Ephesians 5:18-20? _____

_____

_____

_____

e. According to Psalms 22:27, 29 y 86:9, at the end times, who will worship Jehovah, our God? _____

_____

_____

_____

3. What is the purpose of Worship Ministries in my local church?

Worship Ministries should direct the music and spiritual songs, whether they be hymns or choruses, drama, art, mime, etc. in the service to exalt our God, together with the other worship activities of the service, such as prayers, testimonies, Bible readings, offerings, and the sermon. The leaders of Worship Ministries should seek to grow spiritually every day, and be in harmony with the other workers in this ministry and the other brothers and sisters in the church.

In order to achieve this purpose, Worship Ministries should rely upon leaders that seek the presence of God in their lives and present their gifts and abilities to the Lord for Him to use to build up the church. As part of this process, they should organize and rehearse their participation in the services. Through this ministry, its members seek to instruct the whole church in the worship that pleases God and enables them to fulfill their mission in the world.

4. How can this ministry benefit the development of my Christian life?

Through participation in Worship Ministries, you can feel the joy of experiencing the presence of God and hearing his voice speaking to us. Your well-focused participation in this ministry can contribute to the unity and edification of the church as a Body that lives its faith together and is committed to sharing it.

Worship Ministries will help you to be useful in the hands of the Lord and to continue your spiritual growth with the other brothers and sisters at the church. You will be able to see how God will powerfully use your singing, music skills, artistic skills, drama skills, and creativity to lead His people to healthy and genuine worship before Him.

Also, through Worship Ministries you can identify other potential leaders in this ministry and accompany them in the process of their growth and effectiveness in it.

5. How is Worship Ministries developed and led in the local church?

Worship ministries can be developed in the church in various ways, but it must always be coordinated with the liturgy, preaching, and specific ministry that the church is carrying out. In this sense, the pastor should never delegate his/her participation within the Worship Ministries in the organization and focus of worship during the various church services. He or she must have focused input into how everything fits together to help people worship, hear from God, and respond to Him.

Worship can be lead by a worship team that will lead the congregation, a choir that will periodically share spiritual songs, people with special gifts to sing, a band or musical orchestra that will accompany the songs and more, etc. The Ministry of Worship may also include dramatizations, mimes, recitations of poetry and various genres, as well as other expressions that contain a message that leads us to recognize and worship God.

The main thing we want from the Worship Ministries is that, in addition to the special experience of worshiping God together, we can capture a worship lifestyle reflected in everything we do outside the formal worship services. Adoration that pleases God must encourage us to participate in God's mission in the world and to live in ways that draw others to Christ and his church.

Can I be involved in Worship Ministries?

1. Do you have a basic knowledge of what worship is according to the Old and New Testaments?   Yes ☐ No ☐

2. Has God given you musical, singing, artistic, acting, or creative talents? Yes ☐ No ☐

3. Do you enjoy participating in worshiping God with your fellow brothers and sisters in Christ of the Church?   Yes ☐ No ☐

4. Are you available to rehearse and prepare for long hours to offer your best worship to our God? Yes ☐ No ☐

5. Do you consider it important to share the abilities that God has given you in worship with others that are beginning in this ministry?   Yes ☐ No ☐

6. Do you desire to continue training in the techniques and knowledge of music/singing/drama/art/etc. in order to be more effective in planning/leading of public worship?   Yes ☐ No ☐

7. Is it important for you to prepare in prayer in anticipation of the time of worship and each item of the service with all those involved?   Yes ☐ No ☐

8. Are you willing to submit to your pastor and church in order to effectively contribute to the Worship Ministries of your local church? Yes ☐ No ☐

9. Are you committed to the ministry of your local church and support it by attending the services and supporting it financially? Yes ☐ No ☐

10. Do you worship God through your lifestyle and relationships with others even when you are not leading worship in the services? Yes ☐ No ☐

If at least 7 of your answers were "Yes", you could serve your church in Worship Ministries.

Materials you can use to train and inform yourself for these ministries:

* *Grace and Devotion* (Hymnal).

* *The Theology of Worship.* Ralph P. Martin.

* *Come, Let's Worship.* James R. Sprunge.

* *School of Leadership - Basic Courses*

Nazarene Compassionate Ministries

1. What is Nazarene Compassionate Ministries?

Nazarene Compassionate Ministries (NCM) is the ministry of the church that, motivated by the love of Christ, helps us to respond in different ways to the integral needs of people: physical, intellectual, material, relational, and spiritual.

2. Using a Bible, answer the following questions:

a. What is Christian compassion? (Luke 10:33-27) _____

_____

_____

_____

b. Where does my commitment to compassion come from? (1 John 3:16) _____

_____

_____

_____

c. What are two examples of compassion that Jesus gives us in Matthew 14:14 and 15:32?

_____

_____

3. What is the purpose of Nazarene Compassionate Ministries in my local church?

The purpose of Nazarene Compassionate Ministries is to embody the wholistic ministry of the compassion of Christ to the world, meeting the diverse needs of people, and using different methods, such as providing resources, training a network of individuals, and sending them through the church to touch our world in the name of Jesus.

4. How can NCM benefit me in the development of my spiritual life?

a. Rediscovering the Biblical message. Read and comment on 1 John 2:7-9.

b. Performing acts of love like Jesus. Read and comment on Matthew 9:35-36 and Mark 6:35-37.

c. Identifying and involving others who have gifts of compassion. Read and comment on Acts 6:1-5; Romans 12:6-8 and 1 Corinthians 12:28.

5. How is Nazarene Compassionate Ministries developed and carried out in the local church?

Nazarene Compassionate Ministries can be developed by:

a. Using preaching, teaching, and the ministries of the church to train the congregation through bible studies, the exposition of themes related to Christian compassion, and thus discover how the first Christians responded to the physical and material needs of people, and how was can do the same today.

b. Organizing a committee of people interested in this ministry in order to take special action, taking advantage of the capabilities of church members and professionals in the church.

c. Starting to serve those with needs inside of the church, and then extending further out, initially through the relationships of church members with people of the community.

d. Extending service out into the community through participation and coordination with existing service institutions, such as hospitals, firefighters, schools, Non Governmental Organizations (NGO's), among others.

e. Starting special projects of the church in service to the community, like: Children's feeding center, craft workshops, agricultural projects, small business training, and many others that may arise from the particular needs of the community around the church.

Other services that NCM offers to the local church:
- Disaster relief
- Education
- Community development
- Nutrition for children

There are also some events in the life of the community that are conducive to the practice of compassion:

- **Disasters:** Helping people in a time of need is an opportunity to give testimony to the love and transformation of God.

- **AIDS:** This epidemic that is advancing so rapidly gives us a great opportunity to demonstrate God's love to those who suffer.

- **Children:** 50% of the population is composed of children under the age of 18 years. This population group faces large problems, such as malnutrition, abandonment, orphanhood, homelessness, lack of adequate education, security, sex and slave trafficking, among others. Helping children is also a great opportunity to demonstrate God's love in a very tangible way.

Can I be involved in NCM?

1. Helping the poor and needy is a pleasure for me.
   Yes ☐ No ☐

2. It challenges me to find appropriate ways of meeting the needs of people. Yes ☐ No ☐

3. I want to help children, youth, and adults who are in need.
   Yes ☐ No ☐

4. I have participated in some activities of compassion.
   Yes ☐ No ☐

5. I would be willing to sacrifice to meet the needs of those around me. Yes ☐ No ☐

6. When I hear of people out of work who cannot pay their debts, I do what I can to help them. Yes ☐ No ☐

7. I enjoy ministering to people in hospitals, prisons, or nursing homes. Yes ☐ No ☐

8. I feel compassion for people who are lonely or discouraged, and I like to spend time encouraging them. Yes ☐ No ☐

9. I prefer to study sociology rather than theology. Yes ☐ No ☐

10. I think that meeting the physical, material, and social needs of people is a form of showing them Christ's love. Yes ☐ No ☐

If at least 7 of your answers were "Yes", you might be able to serve your church in Nazarene Compassionate Ministries

Materials you can use to train and inform yourself for this ministry:
Participate in the course of Ministry Training. (CC1, CC2)

Books

- *Companion to the Poor.* Viv Grigg. Ed.

- *Walking with the Poor.* Bryant L. Myers.

- *The Greening, the Story of Nazarene Compassionate Ministries.* Steve Weber and Franklin Cook. Ed..

- *School of Leadership - Basic Courses, Compassionate Ministries*

Ministry of Communications

I. What is the Ministry of Communications?

Communications Ministries is a tool that the local church counts on to make good use of the various methods of communication to reach people. This doesn't only refer to radio and television, but also to each method of communication - electronic or not - that can facilitate the completion of the mission of the church of the Lord.

2. Using the Bible, answer the following questions:

a. What form of communications does God tell the prophet to use in Habakkuk 2:2? _____

_____

b. According to Mark 3:14, how were Jesus' 12 chosen disciples going to communicate Jesus' message? _____

_____

_____

c. Which medium did God use in John 20:27-28 so that the apostle Thomas would believe? __

_____

_____

_____

d. What does Matthew 13:3 tells us was the visual medium most used by Jesus in his teachings? _____

_____

e. Where did Paul preach and teach the brothers in Ephesus according the Acts 20:20?_____

3. What is the purpose of Communications in the church?

The purpose of Communications Ministries is to support the church in faithfully proclaiming the message of the gospel and informing people about the ministries of the church. Using this ministry as a valuable tool, the church searches to use all of the mediums of communication to their advantage in order to share the message of salvation and inward holiness, especially to those who don't activity participate in the church.

In the following table, mark with an X the forms of communication that you have observed the local church actually using. Note that these mediums can focus on those inside the church, those outside the church, or both. You can add others in the blank spaces.

X	Toward the Inside	X	Toward the Outside	X	Both
	Ushers (hosts)		Letter with the name of the church and hours of activities		Posters
	Welcome cards		District Bulletin		Local radio broadcasts
	Informative brochure of the ministries of the church		Local newspaper ad about the church		Broadcasts on TV
	Local Church Bulletin		Church in national publications		Church Website
	Bulletin boards		Billboard about the church		Distribution of the Holiness Today magazine
	Worship Service program		Mobile Publicity (bus, etc)		Use of special video or audio during the sermon
	Announcements from the Pulpit		Closed circuit TV ads about the church in supermarkets, etc.		
	Transparencies, Powerpoints, or song sheets with song lyrics.		Personal Invitations		
	Prayer lists		Direct Publicity (house by house)		
	Telephone numbers of members		Distribution of tracts (person to person)		
	Letters to members				
	E-mail				

4. How can this ministry benefit me in the development of my Christian life?

Participating in Communications Ministries in the church helps us to keep actively involved in the mission of God through the ministry of the local church. In this manner, our lives are enriched and we are collaborating with others to build up the saints and save mankind.

This committed participation affects us socially as well as spiritually. We are blessed to work in the Body of Christ with others (1 Corinthians 12:12-26) and we are partners with Jesus in his mission (2 Cor. 5:20).

5. How is this ministry developed in the local Church?

Communications Ministries is very wide and can be developed in many ways. It's very important that you don't wait until you have the latest in equipment before you start this ministry. Start looking around at the needs and consider your abilities and the available resources. For example, start by making an announcement for the next church activity. If your church has a local newsletter or bulletin board, you can work to make it an attractive and effective means of communication. Contact the pastor and the ministry directors of the church to obtain information about their ministries and upcoming activities. Be creative in communicating this to the congregation. Or if such a bulletin doesn't exist, you can create one.

It's important that you think of this ministry as a means, in the Body of Christ, through which God can use you significantly. Therefore, commit yourself to the church and its leaders and take the challenge to go and develop a Communications Ministry in your church. Maybe you will encounter obstacles, but continue moving ahead. God is with you!

Could I get involved in Communications Ministry?

1. I am available to go from house to house through my neighborhood to announce activities of my church. Yes ☐ No ☐

2. I enjoy creating promotional pieces to announce the activities of my church. Yes ☐ No ☐

3. I would like to daily maintain the social networks of my church. Yes ☐ No ☐

4. I can talk in front of unknown people. Yes ☐ No ☐

5. I enjoy writing articles, promos, etc. for the local newspaper. Yes ☐ No ☐

6. I am creative and can develop promotional activities for my local church. Yes ☐ No ☐

7. I think it is crucial that we use the internet, social networks, and all social media to promote the events and ministries of the church. Yes ☐ No ☐

8. I would like to record the Pastor's sermons for others to listen to at later times. Yes ☐ No ☐

9. I also look for resources to help the church be better informed. Yes ☐ No ☐

10. I would like to design a church website so that people could know more about our church and stay better connected. Yes ☐ No ☐

If you answered at least 7 of the questions "yes," you could serve your church in the Ministry of Communications.

Materials that you can use to train yourself in this ministry:
- *School of Leadership - Basic Courses, Course of Communication*

THE MINISTRY OF COMMUNICATIONS CONTINUES WORKING STRENUOUSLY TO CREATE A REGIONAL WEBSITE (MESOAMERICAREGION.ORG) AS A SOURCE OF SUPPORT FOR THE LOCAL CHURCH AND ITS MINISTRIES. WE HAVE AUDIOVISUAL RESOURCES: RADIO PROGRAMS, BOOKS, VIDEOS, VIRTUAL HYMNAL, PHOTOS, NEWS, INTERACTIVE MAP, ETC.!!! AND YOU CAN ACCESS IT FOR FREE !!!

Ministry of
Personal
Discipleship

I. What is the Personal Discipleship Ministry?

Personal Discipleship Ministry in the local church is the comprehensive and intentional training for all of life for those who know Jesus as their Savior. This type of discipleship helps followers of Jesus to start and develop an intimate and growing relationship with Him in order to serve Him and others.

2. Using a Bible, answer the following questions:

a. According to Matthew 10:1, What did Jesus do at the start of his ministry? _____

_____

_____

b. What are the requirements that Jesus sets out in Mark 8:34 for those who want to follow Him?_____

_____

_____

_____

c. According to Luke 6:40, what must be the relationship between Jesus the teacher and his disciples? _____

_____

_____

_____

d. What should characterize the disciples of Jesus, according to John 13:35? _____

_____

_____

e. In Acts 6:7, What happened to the number of disciples in the early church? _____

3. What is the purpose of the Ministry of Personal Discipleship in my local church?

The Personal Discipleship Ministry, under the leadership of Sunday School and Discipleship Ministries (SDMI), and connected to all the other ministries of the church, helps new Christians to be immediately cared for by other more mature brothers and sisters. They will help the new believer become established in his or her new faith and in their new relationship with Jesus. In this way, the fruit of evangelism will be preserved. That means that new Christians will be cared for and taught so that they will not fall away from Christ.

Discipleship helps develop Christians, both new and long-time Christians, with solid foundations in their walk with Christ and committed to the work of God. Thus they can be incorporated into the church as reproductive members and leaders who serve others through their ministry through the church. Dynamic and constant discipleship in the church provides a model for the permanent growth of each believer, and makes it possible for many believers to disciple others, that is, they themselves can become disciplers.

4. How can the Personal Discipleship Ministry help me in the development of my Christian life?

Through participation in the Personal Discipleship Ministry, you can be used by God, since you will be investing your energies, time, knowledge, and resources to guide others in the way of Christ. It will give you great joy to see their growth from week to week, and the changes that God makes in their life and in their relationships with others. Also, you will cultivate a unique relationship of spiritual friendship with him or her and their family.

Another direct result of your participation in the Personal Discipleship Ministry your own spiritual growth. When you teach or share your own spiritual experiences and life with others, you will see that your development and commitment to Christ is accelerated in a special way.

Finally, your participation supports the health, development, and multiplication of your local church. You will experience the great satisfaction of knowing that you are contributing personally to the fulfillment of the mission of the church.

5. How is the Ministry of Personal Discipleship developed and led in my local church?

The development of the Ministry of Personal Discipleship in the local church depends very much on how this ministry has been working. If discipleship as something intentional and organized has not existed, then the church has a double challenge: (1) to disciple the brothers and sisters and (2) to discover, recruit, and empower those who have the gifts, willingness, and time to begin this ministry.

Beyond basic discipleship, the church must develop a system of constant discipleship that leads each person to maturity in Christ. This includes guiding people to active membership in the church, the experience of entire sanctification, the discovery of their spiritual gifts, the ministry that God calls each person, and the realization of a life of service to others.

If you find yourself with the following basic skills for participating in the Ministry of Personal Discipleship in your local church, meet with your pastor or local SDMI leaders to contribute to this very crucial ministry.

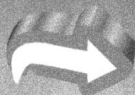

Can I be involved in Personal Discipleship Ministry?

1. Do you have a basic knowledge of the true fundamentals of the Bible? Yes ☐ No ☐

2. Are you interested in contributing to the spiritual growth of others? Yes ☐ No ☐

3. Do you enjoy sharing your Christian testimony since you came to know Christ? Yes ☐ No ☐

4. Do you nourish yourself daily from the Word of God and through prayer for your spiritual growth? Yes ☐ No ☐

5. Have some of the people of the church commented about your ability to teach or guide others in their walk with Christ?
Yes ☐ No ☐

6. Do you want to continue growing in your knowledge of the Word and in ways of helping others mature in their faith?
Yes ☐ No ☐

7. Are you characterized by your consistency and perseverance in all that you do? Yes ☐ No ☐

8. Do you understand new converts and the situations of their lives before Christ? Yes ☐ No ☐

9. Are you committed to the ministry of the local church, and support it with your attendance and financial support? Yes ☐ No ☐

10. Can you use printed materials as a guide, or find other ways to help a person develop in their faith? Yes ☐ No ☐

If at least 7 of your answers were "Yes", you could serve your church in the Personal Discipleship Ministry.

Materials you can use to train and inform yourself for this ministry:

- *A Handbook for Discipleship Training*
- *Basic Discipleship Lessons (New Life in Christ, Keys to an Abundant Christian Life)* for adults. Along with these lessons: *Dictionary for New Believers, Sharing Christ with my Family and Friends, Discovering Jesus every Day, United to the Family of God, What Nazarenes Believe, 4 Steps to being a joyful tither, Receive Power,* and *How to Read the Bible Every Day and Learn from It.*
- *High Voltage Basic Bible Studies for Youth*
- *So you want to follow Jesus* for kids, *Young Believers Discipleship Series*
- *Following Jesus 1, 2, 3*
- *Welcome to the Church of the Nazarene*
- School of Leadership - Basic Courses, Course of Christian Discipleship
- These resources and more can be found at: ***www.discipleship.mesoamericaregion.org***

Ministry of
Evangelism

1. What is the Ministry of Evangelism?

Evangelism Ministry in the church consists of all the efforts made toward reaching others for Christ and incorporating them as a part of the local community of disciples. Following the model of Jesus and assuming his mission (Luke 4:18-19), we are led to develop Biblical strategies and practices that involve all disciples of Jesus in effectively sharing the Gospel to the greatest number of people around us. With this focus, our evangelism will lead us to plant new churches. This is To Be Like Him!

2. Using the Bible, complete the following phrases::

a. In John 3:16, what is God's purpose in sending his Son to the world? _____
_____

b. What did the four friends of the paralytic do in Mark 2:3-4 that reflects what we should do with those who do not have access to Jesus?_____
_____
_____

c. If we see Luke 4:18-19 as the focus for Jesus' evangelism ministry, what are the seven dimensions of this ministry?

1._____

2._____

3._____

4._____

5._____

6._____

7._____

3. What is the purpose of this ministry in my local church?

The purpose of Evangelism Ministry in the local church has several aspects, among which are:

Promoting evangelism and working to conserve the fruit of evangelism.

Being focused on and mobilized to meet the need of salvation in people around us.

Creating and implementing strategies to incorporate evangelism into the total life of the church. Giving an evangelism focus to all the ministries of the church so that we are better able to touch the lives of people with the Gospel of Christ. This focus also will lead to the implementation of district, regional and denominational programs for evangelism.

Guiding the new converts to be trained and then become members of the church who share their faith, reach others for Christ, and are committed to world evangelism, beginning with their participation in their local church.

4. How will this ministry be of benefit to me in the development of my own Christian life?

A Christian life focused on Biblical evangelism will allow us to always see the great needs of others for salvation, and therefore be more committed to participate and promote any means in the local church to accomplish this.

Of course, this lifestyle will affect your spiritual life and subsequently your actions. It will lead to a consecrated Christ-like life, permitting His will to be done in place of yours; a life of prayer and deep compassion for the lost and a life that looks to impact others with the Gospel. And finally, it will permit the training of those who will consistently go to share the good news of salvation with others.

5. How is this ministry developed in the local church?

Every church should have an evangelistic vision that is reflected in the environment and openness of the church to receive and be concerned for new people.

Then the church should be organized so that, as part of its strategy, it can do evangelistic activities through people of different ages and groups in the church to meet the needs of people outside of the church.

To be able to do this, the church must be motivated and constantly trained in the effective use of different means of evangelism. The greatest number and variety possibly of evangelistic methods should be used to include the greatest number of people in the church. See the list at the end.

Could I be involved in Evangelism?

1. Have I led many people to accept Christ?
   Yes ☐ No ☐

2. Am I very concerned about the salvation of others? Yes ☐ No ☐

3. Do I feel guilty when I do not evangelize? Yes ☐ No ☐

4. Can I see myself preaching at an evangelistic campaign?
   Yes ☐ No ☐

5. Do I like to train people to preach? Yes ☐ No ☐

6. Do I want to invest time to learn how to share Jesus with others?
   Yes ☐ No ☐

7. Is sharing the Gospel the most important ministry? Yes ☐ No ☐

8. Can I speak to people about Jesus without being afraid?
   Yes ☐ No ☐

9. Am I concerned when I think that people will go to hell if the Gospel is not shared with them? Yes ☐ No ☐

10. When I share the Gospel, do I sense the power of God?
    Yes ☐ No ☐

If at least 7 of your answers were YES, you could serve your church in the Evangelism Ministry.

Materials that can be used for training in this ministry:
- The Collision Between The Law and Grace (Book)
- EvangeCube and EvangeCards
- Holiness Cube and Holiness Cards
- The Power of the Glorious Church
- Spiritual Expedition (a Spiritual Gift Journey)
- The Jesus Film
- Evangelism Manual
- Jesus Film Manual
- To Be Like Him Manual
- True Hope
- Missional Zone Planter 5

Website: www.mesoamericaregion.org   ¨click¨ Evangelism

Youth Evangelism

I. What is the Youth Evangelism Ministry?

This ministry, as a part of Nazarene Youth International (NYI), and together with the local evangelism ministry, encourages and involves the youth of the church in the work of evangelism. This is done by guiding them to grow in spiritual maturity and reflecting Christ, and developing and equipping them to multiply disciples for the glory of the name of the Lord.

2. Using your Bible, answer the following questions:

a. In Mark 10:21, how did Jesus look at this young man?

_____

_____

_____

b. Describe this young man as he went away after not obeying Jesus? Read Matthew 19:22 and Luke 18:23. _____

_____

_____

_____

c. In contrast to this young man, how did the man in Luke 19:6 respond to Jesus? _____

_____

d. What did Paul ask for in his prayer in Ephesians 6:18-19? _____

_____

_____

3. What is the purpose of the Youth Evangelism Ministry in my local church?

The purpose of the Youth Evangelism Ministry is to guide, develop, and equip young people to be like Christ and complete the Great Commandment (Matthew 22:34-40) and the Great Commission (Matthew 28:18-19), which will produce a Great Transformation in the youth of this present generation.

The challenge is to be like Jesus, and for that, we present the 7 biblical spiritual disciplines that Jesus practiced.

Complete the following sentences:

a. Jesus was c_ _ _ _ _ _ _ _ completely, surrendering his will. (Galatians 2:20).

b. Jesus p_ _ _ _ _ for others (Mark 1:35, Luke 10:21, Luke 6:12).

c. Jesus l_ _ _ _ people and served them with compassion (Matthew 4:23).

d. Jesus p_ _ _ _ _ _ _ _ _ the kingdom of God (Luke 4:18-19).

e. Jesus' purpose was to s _ _ _ and s _ _ _ the lost (Luke19:10).

f. Jesus was an e_ _ _ _ _ _ for his followers (John 13:15).

g. Jesus delegated the m_ _ _ _ _ _ _ to his disciples. (Luke 9:1-2).

This ministry works with the NYI to develop and implement a variety of continuous ministries and events especially to reach youth for Christ.

4. How can this ministry benefit me in the development of my Christian life?

If you are a youth, this ministry will help you share love and compassion with those who still don't know God. It will help you remain committed and invite others to join you in being disciples of Jesus. This type of life, oriented towards others, will help you grow in your life of holiness as a youth in our world.

As an adult, it will be a great blessing for you to be part of a local church that has a vibrant and dynamic youth ministry that focuses on attracting youth to Christ, helping them make Jesus Lord of their lives. You could help disciple them as they make the important decisions that will impact the rest of their lives.

5. How is the Youth Evangelism Ministry developed in my local church?

The Youth Evangelism Ministry is developed in the local church through the organization of Nazarene Youth International (NYI) with its leaders and three ministries of evangelism, discipleship, and leadership.

One valuable tool for effectively carrying out the ministry of Youth Evangelism is the start of youth friendship groups. Bonds of friendship are formed in these groups that contribute to spiritual growth through prayer and the application of God's Word to their lives, and the development of youth leaders. However, the special focus of these groups is to invite non-Christian youth to be a part so that they can experience the love of God and give their lives to Him. Then, these groups grow and divide and continue the same dynamic to reach many youth for Christ.

Could I be involved in Youth Evangelism?

1. The state of the lives of the youth of my community worries me. Yes ☐ No ☐

2. I like to share the message of the gospel with youth. Yes ☐ No ☐

3. It hurts me greatly and I'm worried about how the youth of my community behave. Yes ☐ No ☐

4. I am available to open my home to share with youth who need the Lord. Yes ☐ No ☐

5. I feel the need of training youth in methods of youth evangelism. Yes ☐ No ☐

6. I am committed to discipling new Christian youth in their vital spiritual development. Yes ☐ No ☐

7. I want to continue learning and maturing in my relationship with Christ and others in order to raise up leaders among the youth. Yes ☐ No ☐

8. I want to use who I am and what I have to impact youth for Christ. Yes ☐ No ☐

9. I want to be part of a church with a dynamic growing youth group that seeks out lost youth. Yes ☐ No ☐

10. If the Lord calls me to be an evangelist among the youth, I will accept. Yes ☐ No ☐

If at least 7 of your answers were Yes, you could serve your church in the Ministry of Youth Evangelism.

Materials that can be used for training in this ministry:
Resources:
• Workshop of Sex, Lies, and the Truth

• Camp: Evangelism in action

• Evangelism Cube

• Jesus Film

• *School of Leadership - Basic Courses, Youth Ministry, Evangelism*

Website:
www.mesoamericaregion.org/es/jni

Nazarene Youth International

1. What is the ministry of Nazarene Youth International (NYI)?

NYI is the ministry of the Church of the Nazarene that exists in order to reach and guide youth toward a relationship with God that lasts their whole life. Also, it is a group of Nazarene youth worshiping, serving, growing, working, and having fun together.

The NYI is formed by all of the youth of the church and people young at heart who want to evangelize and disciple youth. Even if there are no youth in your church, the NYI has a reason to exist: to reach youth for Christ!

2. Using the Bible, answer the following questions:

a. One of the verses that gives strength and sustenance to the ministry of NYI is 1 Timothy 4:12. According to this text, in what areas are youth invited to be an example?

1. _____ 2. _____

3. _____ 4. _____

5. _____ 6. _____

b. All of the NYI activities have a purpose:
   To make _____ of Jesus (Matthew 28:19-20).
c. Youth Ministry has a clear and defined goal. Based on Colossians 1:28, what is the goal of youth ministry? Present every youth fully m_ _ _ _ _ in C_ _ _ _ _.

3. What is the purpose of NYI in my local church?

There are over 150 million youth in Latin America and the Caribbean. However, the vast majority of them don't have a personal relationship with Jesus. Hence the importance of an integrated ministry for youth and young adults that calls their generation to live a dynamic life in Christ. Jesus tells us that as his disciples, we are the S_ _ _ and the L_ _ _ _ of the world in which we live (Matthew 5:13-16).

On the other hand, once a youth has received Jesus as his or her personal savior, it's important that they find an atmosphere that helps them in their spiritual growth. This atmosphere is provided by the NYI as a ministry and as groups of friends. According to Ephesians 4:15-16, to what are Christians compared, and what must we do?

_____

_____

_____

_____

4. How can NYI help me in the development of my Christian life?

A. If you are a youth, you will find in the NYI help from adults and other youth who have decided to follow Jesus, and have experienced, or are experiencing situations similar to yours.
B. If you are an adult and have the desire to help youth, the NYI provides you with the opportunity of serving them.
C. In addition, belonging to the NYI allows you to take on, along with other youth, the challenge of reaching youth for Christ.

5. How is NYI developed in the local church?

The NYI Ministry is developed around these core points:

Youth Evangelism: NYI develops and implements a variety of ongoing ministries and special events to reach youth for Christ.

Discipleship: NYI develops and implements a variety of ongoing ministries and special events to build up and challenge youth to grow as disciples of Christ in personal devotion, worship, fellowship, ministry, and guiding others toward Christ.

Leadership: NYI develops and implements a variety of ongoing ministries and special events to guide and train youth to become leaders for Christ and His church.

There are a large variety of resources that the NYI ministry can use. In reality, the only limit is the creativity of the leaders of the church. Here are some resources and programs that can be of great use in your church.

In the Name of Jesus - Program of prayer for the development of a life of prayer among the youth.

Sex, lies, and the truth - A program for strengthening the character of youth based on the biblical perspective of sexuality.

Maximum Mission - A program for mobilizing everyone who wants to develop their gifts and talents through short term missions trips.

Youth Bible Quizzing - A fun and exciting program that challenges youth to a permanent life of Bible study and obedience to the Word of God.

Youth Pastor Diploma - A program designed to prepare someone to serve as a youth pastor and lead the youth ministry of a local church.

Could I be a part of the NYI Ministry?

1. I'm at ease communicating with youth. Yes ☐ No ☐

2. It excites me when I see youth and young adults accept Christ as their Savior. Yes ☐ No ☐

3. I like to help in activities for youth and young adults, even if I must keep myself awake. Yes ☐ No ☐

4. I like to minister to youth and young adults with modern music. Yes ☐ No ☐

5. I like to help as a counselor at youth camps. Yes ☐ No ☐

6. I want to help in the formation of new leaders among the youth. Yes ☐ No ☐

7. I am convinced that youth have a place of service in the church. Yes ☐ No ☐

8. I motivate youth to evangelize other youth. Yes ☐ No ☐

9. I have been a leader of youth and/or young adults. Yes ☐ No ☐

10. I am interested in helping youth, not only in their spiritual lives, but also in other areas of their lives. Yes ☐ No ☐

If at least 7 of your answers were YES, you could serve your church in the ministry of Nazarene Youth International.

Materials that you can use to train yourself in this ministry:

- Diploma in Youth Ministry from the Youth Ministry Academy, DiscipleshipPlace.org
- Call Waiting - Discover Your Call and Connect with the Life of Passion and Greatness that God Has Tailor-Made For You, Mesoamerica Region Discipleship Ministries
- Reactive Manual, Training for Youth Leadership. 2015
- Choose Life - A Guide for Peer Educators and Youth Leaders
- Guide books for Youth Bible Quizzing.
- A Handbook for Discipleship Training, Mesoamerica Region Discipleship Ministries
- School of Leadership - Basic Courses, Youth Ministry Courses
- High Voltage Basic Discipleship Lessons for Youth. Mesoamerica Region Literature

Sunday School and Discipleship Ministries International

> ## I. What is Sunday School and Discipleship Ministries International (SDMI)?
>
> Sunday School and Discipleship Ministries International helps us fulfill the Grand Commission, serving children, youth, and adults to prepare them for a life of Christian holiness. SDMI is important in the educational ministries of the church. The ministries that make up SDMI are divided into three categories:
>
> a. **Children's Ministries:** Sunday School, discipleship, camps, Bible Quizzing, Children's Church, Vacation Bible School, Sports Ministries, Special Needs Ministries (Gift of Love), Caravans, etc.
>
> b. **Youth Ministries:** Sunday School, Discipleship, Leadership Development, Special Needs Ministries (Gift of Love), Sports Ministries, etc.
>
> c. **Adult Ministries:** Sunday School/Small Groups, Personal Discipleship, Senior Adult Ministries, Women's Ministries, Men's Ministries, Marriage Ministries, Special Needs Ministries, Single Adults Ministries, Leadership Development,
>
> ## 2. Using the Bible, answer the following questions:
>
> a. What is Jesus' command in Matthew 28:20? _____
> _____
> _____

b. According to Mark 1:22, What drew the attention of Jesus' teaching? _____
_____

c. Read Luke 18:9-30. Circle one or more of the options for each question below:

To whom is Jesus teaching in vv. 9-14?
      Adults   Youth   Children
To whom is Jesus teaching in vv. 15-17?
      Adults   Youth   Children
To whom is Jesus teaching in vv. 18-30?
      Adults   Youth   Children

d. Who were the first teachers in the church according to Acts 2:42?_____

3. What is the purpose of SDMI in my local church?
The purpose of SDMI has four parts:
a. To be a people of prayer, engaged in The Word, making Christlike disciples.
b. To intentionally develop relationships with unreached people so that they become Christlike disciples making Christlike disciples.
c. To teach the Word of God to children, youth, and adults so that they are saved, sanctified wholly, and maturing in Christian experience that results in a life of compassion, evangelism, Christian education, and disciple making.
d. To encourage everyone to faithfully engage in a discipleship ministry such as Sunday School/Bible studies, small groups, and other disciple-making ministries.

4. How can SDMI benefit me in the development of my Christian life?
a. The heart of SDMI is the Sunday School and Small Groups where each week people receive solid biblical teaching from a teacher/leader, together with other brothers and sisters of similar physical or spiritual age. Through these

classes/groups, people are nurtured by the Word and discover how to apply the learned principles to their daily lives, and grow in communion and friendship with each other. The students and the teachers are impacted in such a support group.

b. Also the Sunday School and Small Groups provide opportunities for children, youth, and adults to learn and invite their friends, no matter their age, to receive teaching from the Bible. This ministry assures that you can continue growing as a faithful disciple of Jesus throughout your whole life.

c. The other ministries of SDMI give people the opportunity to grow together as children, youth, married couples, men, women, and senior adults through different activities of learning by ages, life stage, interests, needs, etc. And as a person grows, if he or she feels God's call to teach or lead, they could be a teacher and/or lead one of these ministries.

5. How is SDMI developed and led in the local church?

SDMI is directed by a council that is in charge of the Christian Education and discipleship program in the local church, with certain rights, obligations, and responsibilities. This council is accountable to the local Church Board. One of its primary functions is to organize the Sunday School and Small Groups by selecting and training the teachers of each class and collecting/raising funds for materials for this ministry.

As we have already seen, there are many other ministries that can take place in the church under the leadership of SDMI, but these depend on the leaders that we have available and on the specific needs of our church and community.

SDMI is a core ongoing ministry of the local church. We should participate in it and continue expanding and improving all aspects of this ministry. It is essential to have in the church a ministry of teaching and discipleship that embraces all the ages (physical and spiritual) of the people who attend.

Could I be involved in SDMI?

1. I am committed to Christian Education for all ages. Yes ☐ No ☐

2. I understand that the church can reach people through the different ministries of SDMI. Yes ☐ No ☐

3. I have discovered that I have the ability and disposition to teach and/or lead. Yes ☐ No ☐

4. I am convinced that nurturing people with the Word of God helps them grow spiritually. Yes ☐ No ☐

5. I can disciple new Christians. Yes ☐ No ☐

6. I consider it necessary to continue growing and updating myself on effective teaching methods. Yes ☐ No ☐

7. I am able to prepare materials to teach classes. Yes ☐ No ☐

8. I enjoy facilitating learning in groups, whether they are children, youth, or adults. Yes ☐ No ☐

9. Together with my wife or husband, we love to help other married couples. Yes ☐ No ☐

10. I am available to participate in planning and evaluation meetings for SDMI. Yes ☐ No ☐

If at least 7 of your answers were "Yes", you could serve your church in the Ministries of Sunday School and Discipleship International (SDMI).

Materials you can use to train and inform yourself for these ministries:

- Manual Church of the Nazarene, Section 812 and following
- Manuals of organization of: VBS (Vacation Bible School), Children's Church, Bible Quizzing, Children's Camps, Evangelism of Children, Women's Ministries, Men's Ministries, Senior Adults (Plenty of Life), Single Adults, Special Needs (Gift of Love), Married Ministry, etc.
- Basic Discipleship for children: So you Want to Follow Jesus?, Young Believers Discipleship Series
- Basic Discipleship for youth: High Voltage, Basic Discipleship Lessons, a Voyage in the Right Direction, etc.
- Basic Discipleship for adults: Basic Discipleship Lessons (New Life in Christ, Keys for an abundant Christian Life), Following Jesus 1,2,3, etc.
- School of Leadership - Basic Courses, Courses of Christian Discipleship
- These resources and more at: **www.discipleship.mesoamericaregion.org**

Nazarene Missions International

1. What is the Ministry of Nazarene Missions International (NMI)?

In essence, NMI is the heart of the Global Mission in every church around the world. It's related to all the structural levels of the church (local, regional and global) and it works under the direction of the district, regional, and global leadership.

2. Answer each question using your Bible:

a. In the Old Testament (Genesis 12:1-3), God called Abraham to start a great nation that was _____ to all the families of the world.

b. After his resurrection, Jesus commanded his disciples (Matthew 28:19-20) to _____ and make disciples of _____ _____, baptizing them in the name of the Father, the Son, and the Holy Spirit.

c. According to Acts 1:8, before Jesus ascended to heaven, he told his disciples that they would receive the power of the Holy Spirit to be his witnesses in J_____, J_____, S_____ and to the ends of the _____.

d. The revelation that God gave to John in Revelations 5:9 states that the gospel is for everyone and that the blood of Jesus Christ can redeem people of every T_____ y L_____ y P_____ y N_____.

3. What is the purpose of NMI in my local church?

There are four 4 strategic objectives: Praying , Discipling, Giving and Educating.

a) PRAYING unites us to "Intercede for leaders and churches, and for the Holy Spirit to draw all people to Christ."

b) DISCIPLING challenge us in "Involving and mentoring future missions leaders, especially youth and children, to make Christlike disciples for God's mission in the nations."

c) EDUCATING: We are responsible for "Informing people of the world's needs and enabling our church to meet those needs in Christ."

d) GIVING: as a member of the local church, we are responsible for "Devoting ourselves and our resources, especially to the World Evangelism Fund, to extend Christ's kingdom." As members of a missionary church, we must support the missionary work of the Nazarene Church, not only with our service but also with our offerings too.

4. How can NMI help me develop my Christian life?

a. It will increase your involvement in interceeding for the world and its need for salvation. Prayer is the thread that unites us with God, not only for asking for what we need, but especially for people to come to know Jesus.

b. You will acquire knowledge about what is going on "out there" on the mission field. Being involved in mission education, you will be able to more intelligently pray, disciple, and give.

c. You will be receiving the challenge, and passing on the challenge, of responding to God's call to the mission field. NMI is responsible for the development of new missions leaders through missionary education.

d. You will better learn to dedicate yourself and your resources for the sending and support of missionaries all around the world, sharing the gospel of salvation with many people.

5. How is NMI developed in my local church?

The local Nazarene Missions International will be an organization of the local church, operating in cooperation with the pastor and the church board through the local NMI Council. This Council will be formed as such:

In churches with more than 100 active members, the annual meeting will elect a minimum of 6 members of the council: president, vice president, secretary, treasurer and two other members. In churches with fewer than 100 active members, the annual meeting must choose a minimum of four members. The selected leaders will begin their work the first day of the new church year after the voting. Churches with fewer than 50 active members must elect two leaders: a president and a vice president. The responsibility of the leaders will be to coordinate activities and to promote the following 12 Emphases in order to achieve the purposes of the ministry in the local church (one for each month):

Every Month	Prayer and Fasting
January	Voluntary Missionaries
February	Alabaster Offering
March	Missionary Education
April	Easter Offering
May	Missionary Care
June	World Missions Broadcast
July	International Ministries/Bible Schools/Seminaries
August	LINKS
September	Alabaster Offering
October	Missions - Priority One
November	Thanksgiving Offering
December	Compassionate Ministries Offering

Should I be a part of this ministry?

1. I pray and fast for the salvation of others.   Yes ☐   No ☐

2. I want to learn about the ministry of Nazarene Missions International (NMI). Yes ☐   No ☐

3. I like to learn about the work of the Church of the Nazarene around the world and share that with the members of my local church.   Yes ☐   No ☐

4. I regularly pray for the missionaries and pastors around the world who preach the Word of God.   Yes ☐   No ☐

5. I am available to give my resources, and motivate my local church to give, so that others can go and take the gospel to the ends of the world. Yes ☐   No ☐

6. I enjoy teaching others about what is happening in the work of missionaries around the world.   Yes ☐   No ☐

7. I am available to motivate people in my local church to be an active part in the recruitment, training, sending, and supporting of national missionaries. Yes ☐   No ☐

8. I always do what I can to share with others what the Church of the Nazarene is doing around the world.   Yes ☐   No ☐

9. I am always interested when someone preaches or teaches about missions. Yes ☐   No ☐

10. I think that missions is the heart of the church. Yes ☐   No ☐

If at least 7 of your answers were Yes, you could serve your church in Nazarene Missions International.

Materials that can be used to train in this ministry:
- *International Missions Education*
- Monthly NMI Missions Videos
- Holiness Today magazines
- Yearly Missionary books (2 for adults and youth, 2 for children)
- *School of Leadership - Basic Courses, Courses of Cross Cultural Missions*

Ministry of Global Mission MAR

1. What is Global Mission MAR (GMMAR)?

Global Mission MAR (Mesoamerica Region) is a ministry that aims to discover, develop and deploy missionaries and leaders from our countries, working as a link between local churches and our global system. This ministry provides the church comprehensive short-term mission experiences and when people discover a call to missions, they receive guidance, training and have the opportunity to participate in other missions trips.

2. Using a Bible, answer the following questions:

a) According to Matthew 28:18-20; Acts 1:8 and John 17:18-20, who was commanded to accomplish the mission?

_____

1. Pastors and missionaries
2. Each disciple
3. Those who already have good training and education

b) Following the example of Noah and Abraham, when God calls us to do something, how should we respond? (Genesis 6:9-22; Genesis 12:1-9; Hebrews 11:7-8)? ____

_____

_____

GLOBAL MISSION
MESOAMERICA

c) God always blesses us so that we can be a
_____ to others. (Genesis 12:1-3)

d) According to Acts 1:8, what do we need in order to be witnesses? _____

_____

e) Jesus' command is to be witnesses in: J_____,
J_____, S_____ and to the e_____

_____.

3. What is the purpose of Global Mission in my local church?

GMMAR exists as a response to the Great Commission expressed in Matthew 28:19-20 to "go and make disciples of all nations..." The Church of the Nazarene has recognized that one way to fulfill this mandate is sending missionaries to all cultures. With the support of NMI, GMMAR exists to share this missional vision with every Nazarene member; in the local church, each person can participate in investing in missions by praying, giving and going.

4. How can Global Mission help me in the development of my Christian life?

a) GMMAR helps you focus on the needs of others. As Christians we were not created to focus on ourselves. God has a bigger plan. Philippians 2:4 says, "not looking to your own interests but each of you to the interests of the others." Read 2 Corinthians 8:1-15. Focus especially on verse two. Even when we think we do not have many resources and that we live in poverty and scarcity, God is calling us to follow the example of the church in Macedonia and cheerfully give to others!

b) GMMAR can motivate you to become involved in missions. Many of us know that mission and ministry around the world are important. We need a way to help us get out of our church buildings and take the gospel to our neighborhood, country and world. In addition to praying and giving, fulfilling the Great Commission means intentional involvement, going with your own hands and feet. Mission is not only for missionaries, it is for the whole church.

c) GMMAR provides a structure for developing and deploying missionaries to cross-cultural ministry. Until recently, our denomination had not developed a system in which a person with a missionary call could become a missionary in the Church of the Nazarene from our countries. Currently it is possible. If you - or someone you know - has a cross-cultural missionary call or a desire to participate in this ministry, GMMAR provides a way to respond to this call.

5. How is Global Mission developed in the local church?

a) Support and get involved in your local church through NMI and the ministry of GM in your district. GMMAR cannot accomplish any of its goals and objectives if people in our churches are not getting involved in NMI and supporting GM on the district level.

b) Participate in Maximum Mission or other group mission trips. How do we learn to play football or draw? By reading a book about it? Watching others to see how they do it? NO! Reading and observing may help, but learning how to play football or draw requires practice. In the same way, talking and reading about missions can help, but you also need to personally experience the mission field to have a broader view of missions.

c) GMMAR provides materials and information about cross-cultural ministry. GMMAR has resources to develop children, youth and adults in missions. Tools include training weekends (Cross-Cultural Orientation or CCO), textbooks, manuals about missions and opportunities to participate in cross-cultural ministry in both short and long term experiences (Maximum Mission, Called to Serve, Genesis, etc.). If you are interested in learning more about these materials, please contact us at the regional office: misionglobal@mesoamericaregion.org

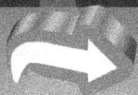

Could I get involved in this ministry?

1. I have a burning desire in my heart to help people in need around the world   Yes ☐ No ☐

2. I feel a call to serve cross-culturally. Yes ☐ No ☐

3. I would be willing to participate in short-term mission trips. Yes ☐ No ☐

4. I am willing to invest time studying in order to fulfill my missionary call more effectively   Yes ☐ No ☐

5. I have lived or traveled in other countries or cultures different from mine and I would be willing to adapt to another culture. Yes ☐ No ☐

6. I am convinced that God calls all Christians to fulfill the Great Commission.   Yes ☐ No ☐

7. I want to teach children and young people about other cultures and missions. Yes ☐ No ☐

8. I am willing to share in churches about missions and to raise funds for missionary ministry.   Yes ☐ No ☐

9. I would go to another country to answer the call of God, knowing that I'd have to leave my own comfort, family and homeland. Yes ☐ No ☐

10. I believe that the culture of my country is not superior to any other culture. Yes ☐ No ☐

If at least 7 of your answers were YES, you should consider participating in the ministry of Global Mission. Contact your district coordinator for more information on how to begin.

Materials to be used for training in this ministry

- *Discovering Missions.* Dr. Charles Gailey. Beacon Press, Kansas City, MO. 2007

- *School of Leadership - Basic Courses, Missions Specialty.* Mesoamerica Region. 2013.

- *Mission in the Third Millennium*. Dr. Charles Gailey. NPH, Kansas City, MO. 2001

- *Maximum Mission Manual.*

Pastoral Ministry

I. What is Pastoral Ministry?

Pastoral Ministry is a vocation (or calling), and at the same time, a special ability that God gives to some members of the Body of Christ, placing under their responsibility and care the well-being and spiritual development of a group of believers for a time.

Studies on this subject show that one of each eight Christians committed to God has the pastoral gift. That means that in a congregation of 50 people, about 6 could be developed for this ministry. It is the reason that healthy and growing churches have specific pastoral ministries for distinct groups of people (Pastors of children, youth, families; Worship Pastors; Educational Pastors, among others).

People called to this ministry are endowed by God with the spiritual gifts that they need to cultivate for the effective development of pastoral ministry. Among these special abilities of the Spirit is the gift of teaching, since the focus of the New Testament on the Pastoral Ministry is to "equip the saints for the work of ministry." (Ephesians 4:12).

2. Using a Bible, answer the following questions:

a. According to Matthew 9:36, What is the description that Jesus gave of the multitudes that did not have the guidance of shepherds (pastors)? _____

_____

b. Read the parable of "The Good Shepherd" in John 10. What are the characteristics that are mentioned there of a good pastor? __

_____

_____

c. Read Acts 4:23 and 1 Timothy 4:1-16 and respond: What is the biblical model of the qualities and responsibilities of pastors?

_____

_____

_____

d. How should pastors care for the congregation of God, according to 1 Peter 5:2-3? _____

_____

3. What is the purpose of Pastor Ministry in my local church?

The purpose of Pastoral Ministry in the local church has many dimensions, including:

a. Evangelizing unbelievers, take care of believers, feed them from the Word of God, and watch over their overall health and growth toward spiritual maturity (Colossians 1:28, 1 Timothy 3:5). This care should be motivated by a deep love for people, just as Christ loves the church (Ephesians 5:22-33).

b. Guiding the church under the direction of the Holy Spirit. However, the work of the pastor is not to do all the work him or herself, but rather to channel the strengths and abilities of the people under his responsibility in order to serve God and others through the different ministries (1 Corinthians 12:28).

4. How can Pastoral Ministry benefit me in the development of my Christian life?

a. In your spiritual growth and maturity: By taking responsibility for the spiritual progress of other people, we identify ourselves with the ministry of Jesus, and continue his work. He invested his life in developing a group of disciples and has entrusted us to continue with that task (Matthew 28:18-20). When we are responsible for the growth of others, we also commit ourselves to our own spiritual growth and maturity. This is because we need to learn more and more in order to always have teaching to give. We need to deepen our relationship with God because we are an example of holiness for others. We need to improve our character, and we do that while we relate to those we are discipling. We grow in the discipline of prayer as we intercede for our disciples, for example.

b. Giving yourself happiness and fulfillment: You will be investing your life and talents in a task that, like no other, contributes to the permanent transformation of the lives of people. When we help build lives and families in the image of Christ, we are contributing to the happiness of people in this life and for all eternity.

5. How is Pastoral Ministry developed in my local church?

Those who want to be involved in Pastoral Ministry will need a lot of training and learning through classes, and learning from others in the ministry. It is important to take advantage of the opportunities offered through the Church of the Nazarene, such as: courses in the local church and seminaries, books and other materials, etc., in order to be trained at the best possible level to prepare for this ministry. Pastoral Ministry in the local church should train and involve the lay people in the ministry. Some areas of ministry where the laity can minister are:

a. Discipling new converts and long-time believers, helping them on their journey of spiritual maturity in Christ.
b. Leading a small Bible Study group in their home or other place (cell group that helps people to grow spiritually), serving in the community, and winning others to Christ.
c. Participating in Pastoral Ministry to a specific group in the church, such as for children, youth, single mothers, married couples, senior adults, among others.
d. Helping the Senior Pastor as an assistant pastor.
e. Planting a new church mission, together with the church board or district church planting team.
f. Teaching a Sunday School class and pastoring the students.

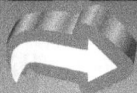

Can I be involved in Pastoral Ministry?

1. I like to help other Christians grow in their spiritual life.
Yes ☐ No ☐

2. It makes me happy to help others overcome the problems that arise in their Christian life. Yes ☐ No ☐

3. It deeply grieves me that some Christians are left without spiritual assistance. Yes ☐ No ☐

4. I'm interested in helping others discover their gifts.
Yes ☐ No ☐

5. I like to spend time in getting to know other Christians and developing a friendship with them. Yes ☐ No ☐

6. People often thank me for the words of encouragement that they receive from me. Yes ☐ No ☐

7. When I preach or teach, people comment that it helps them in their lives as Christians. Yes ☐ No ☐

8. People frequently come to me when they have different needs, because they know that I care about their well-being.
Yes ☐ No ☐

9. When I work with a group of Christians, I am often the one who organizes and leads the other members. Yes ☐ No ☐

10. People follow me as a spiritual leader. Yes ☐ No ☐

If at least 7 of your answers were "Yes", you might be able to serve your church in the Pastoral Ministry.

Materials you can use to train and inform yourself for this ministry:

* *Appreciate People: Effective leadership through effective relationships.* John Maxwell.
* *The pastor as Spiritual Guide.* Howard Rice. Ed. Portavoz, Grand Rapids.
* *The Principle of Interpersonal Relationships.* Stan Toler, Ed. NPH, USA.
* *A Handbook for Discipleship Training.* Ramon Sierra
* *The dynamics of Discipleship Training.* Gary W. Kuhne. Nashville.
* *Making Church Relevant.* Dale Galloway. Ed. USA.
* *Spiritual Leadership.* Oswald Sanders. Ed
* *School of Leadership - Ministerial Leadership*

Work and Witness

I. What is the Ministry of Work and Witness?

The Ministry of Work and Witness (W&W) collaborates in the construction of key physical facilities to carry out the ministry of the church. On many occasions, and according to the needs of the work in the country, local or foreign teams carry out different types of coordinated projects. Many times, those projects include the construction of church buildings.

2. Using a Bible, answer the following questions:

Although the church in the New Testament did not have their own church buildings at first, from the Old Testament we see that the meeting places for the people of God were important.

a. In I Chronicles 22:11, what is the charge that David gives his son Solomon? _____
_____
_____

b. Where does Luke 2:27 tell us that the parents of the baby Jesus took him and then Simeon blessed him? _____
_____

c. In addition to the outdoors, in what other place did Jesus carry out his ministry, according to Matthew 4:23? _____

_____

_____

d. After Paul's conversion in Acts 9:20, where did he usually go to share the gospel? _____

_____

3. What is the purpose of Work and Witness in my local church?

The purpose of W&W in the local church is closely linked with the ministry of the stewards, who are concerned with the maintenance and construction of adequate church buildings, and Nazarene Missions International (NMI), which leads our outreach efforts to other communities and countries. The structures that are built are mainly sanctuaries, class rooms, and pastoral homes.

When a local church, working through our church leadership network, receives help from a group of volunteers from outside their local church, it is to help advance the work of the congregation, not to do all the work for them. The brothers and sisters who come for a short time donate their time, travel expenses, their work, and construction materials.

In addition to doing construction, it is very common that the group participates in other ministries as well, such as Vacation Bible School for the children, Jesus Film projects, Compassionate Ministry projects, etc., all to help people know and follow Jesus.

The purpose of this ministry effort is to contribute to the facilities and ministries of a local church, but more importantly, to encourage the Christian brothers and sisters of that church by offering their skills, attention, and resources for construction in two ways: 1) completion or work toward the completion of the church's own project that they have already started, and

2) be able to organize, maybe together with more churches, to help in the construction of other churches in need.

4. How can Work and Witness help me in the development of my Christian life?

Your participation in W&W can help you in the development of your walk with Christ by giving you opportunities to put use your abilities and willingness to help a church. It is one way of showing your commitment and love to your brothers and sisters and to those you don't know.

In addition, it is a great way of giving to others with joy and sacrifice; this builds you up spiritually. Also, it will give you a lot of satisfaction in doing your part when you see buildings built with suitable places to carry out ministry for people in need.

5. How is W&W developed in the local church?

Work and Witness can be carried out in the church through the committee of stewards or a local committee of construction for a project at your church, or through Nazarene Missions International (NMI) for a project outside of your church. The important thing is to start encouraging the brothers and sisters to give of their economic resources, and challenge them to participate in the project to the extent of their abilities.

In addition, leaders who work directly in this ministry in your country could be asked to give educational workshops or show how W&W teams function. Then you can ask for a team to come help you with your project, or you can put together a team and go help another church with their project. The crucial thing is the commitment and active involvement by the majority of the brothers and sisters in the church.

Can I be involved in Work and Witness?

1. Do you have some construction skills or willingness to learn them? Yes ☐ No ☐

2. Are you available to give of your time to help paint, clean, or repair the church? Yes ☐ No ☐

3. Do you see the need for your church or other churches to have adequate facilities to carry out its ministry? Yes ☐ No ☐

4. Are you interested in the beauty and upkeep of the physical building(s) of your church? Yes ☐ No ☐

5. Can you help with a campaign to collect funds for the construction or addition to your church, or for construction of a church for other people? Yes ☐ No ☐

6. Are you able to manage resources, look for good prices and motivate volunteer workers? Yes ☐ No ☐

7. Is it easy for you to recruit people to donate their time and energies for the work of the church? Yes ☐ No ☐

8. Have you had experience in construction and is it something you enjoy? Yes ☐ No ☐

9. Do you know, or would you be interested to learn, the basic procedures of the law that are needed to be done for construction? Yes ☐ No ☐

10. Are you interested to going to other churches to help them build or repair their church building(s), or help them with other ministry project in their community? Yes ☐ No ☐

If at least 7 of your answers were "Yes", you might be able to serve your church in the ministry of Work and Witness.

Materials you can use to train and inform yourself for this ministry:
- *On Being a Servant of God.* Warren W. Wiersbe.
- *Blue Collar Christianity - Love With Its Sleeves Rolled Up.* Richard Exley. USA.
- *Improving Your Serve.* Charles R. Swindoll
- *School of Leadership - Basic Courses*
- **http://workandwitness.nazarene.org/**

Name of Local Church

This certifies that:

Name

Participated in and satisfactorily completed the course of Basic Lessons of Ministries

CHURCH OF THE
NAZARENE

Local Church Pastor   Discipler

Place and date

www.ingramcontent.com/pod-product-compliance
Lightning Source LLC
Chambersburg PA
CBHW060723030426
42337CB00017B/2992